W9-AAD-942

Fun
Experiments
with
Electricity

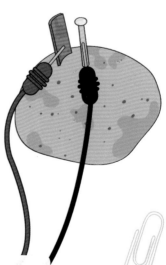

Orange County Library System
146A Madison Rd.
Orange, VA 22960
(540) 672-3811 www.ocplva.org

Provided as a generous gift
of the Orange County
Library Foundation

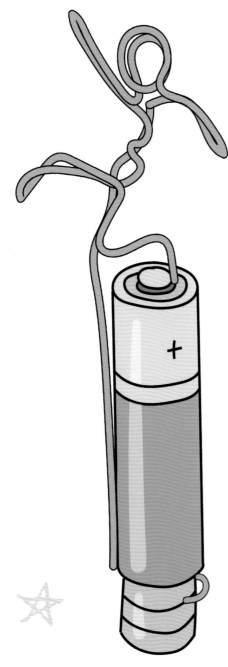

Thanks to the creative team:
Senior Editor: Alice Peebles
Fact checking: Tom Jackson
Design: www.collaborate.agency

Original edition copyright 2017 by Hungry Tomato Ltd.
Copyright © 2018 by Lerner Publishing Group, Inc.

Hungry Tomato® is a trademark of Lerner Publishing
Group, Inc.

Hungry Tomato®
A division of Lerner Publishing Group, Inc.
241 First Avenue North
Minneapolis, MN 55401 USA

For reading levels and more information, look up
this title at www.lernerbooks.com.

Main body text set in Minya Nouvelle Regular 12/15.

The publisher and the author shall not be liable for
any damages allegedly arising from the information
in this book, and they specifically disclaim any liability
from the use or application of any of the contents
of this book. Readers should follow all instructions
and warnings for each experiment in this book and
consult with a parent, teacher, or other adult before
conducting any of the experiments in this book.

Library of Congress Cataloging-in-Publication Data

The Cataloging-in-Publication Data for *Fun Experiments
with Electricity* is on file at the Library of Congress.
ISBN 978-1-5124-3219-0 (lib. bdg.)
ISBN 978-1-5124-4996-9 (EB pdf)

Manufactured in the United States of America
1-41774-23535-4/12/2017

Fun
Experiments
with
Electricity

by Rob Ives
Illustrated by Eva Sassin

HUNGRY
TOMATO®
Minneapolis

Safety First

Take care and use good sense with these amazing science experiments—some are very simple, while others are trickier.

Each project includes a list of everything you will need. Most of the items are things you can find around the house, or they are things that are readily available and inexpensive to buy.

Be sure to check out the Amazing Science behind the projects and learn the scientific principles involved in each experiment.

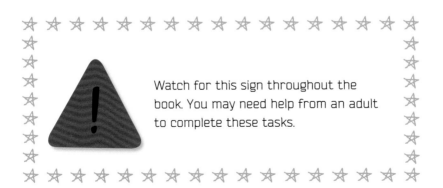

Watch for this sign throughout the book. You may need help from an adult to complete these tasks.

Contents

Electricity

Did you know that even though electricity is one of the basic forces in the universe, scientists only really discovered it a few centuries ago? And when they did, they thought electricity was so amazing that it must be what makes us alive. That's why Frankenstein's monster was brought to life with a zap of lightning—natural electricity. Now you can make your very own mini lightning flash and ten other fun projects sparked by electricity.

You'll see how to turn a toothbrush into a robot, how to make a magnet you can switch on and off, and how to make a flashlight to light your way. You'll even discover how to make your own electricity. Prepare to charge!

You Will need:

Potatoes x3

Balloons

Glass jars with plastic lids

Strip of cardstock

Tissue paper

Copper pieces

Plastic egg

Toothbrush

Kitchen foil

4 inches (10 cm) stiff wire

20-gauge (0.8 mm) uncoated brass wire

22-gauge (0.2 mm²) insulated hook-up wire, red and black

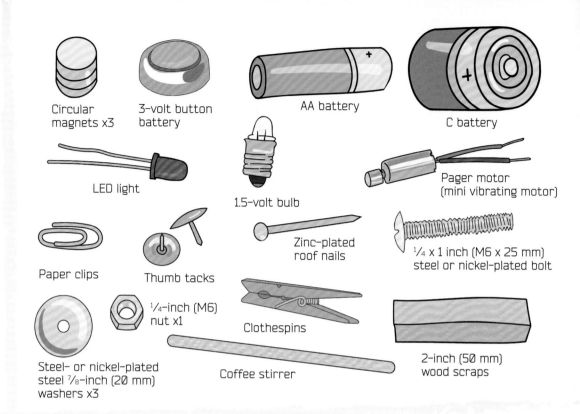

Circular
magnets x3

3-volt button
battery

AA battery

C battery

LED light

1.5-volt bulb

Pager motor
(mini vibrating motor)

Paper clips

Thumb tacks

Zinc-plated
roof nails

$1/4$ x 1 inch (M6 x 25 mm)
steel or nickel-plated bolt

Steel- or nickel-plated
steel $7/8$-inch (20 mm)
washers x3

$1/4$-inch (M6)
nut x1

Clothespins

Coffee stirrer

2-inch (50 mm)
wood scraps

What Tools Will I Need?

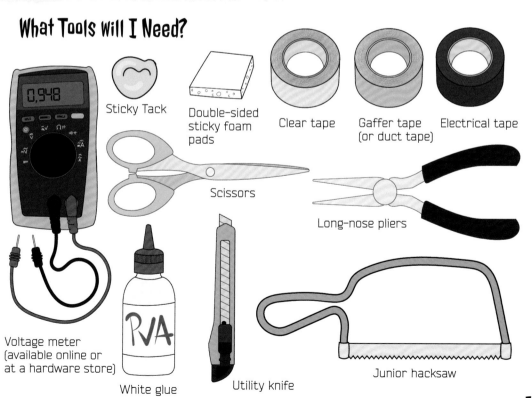

Sticky Tack

Double-sided
sticky foam
pads

Clear tape

Gaffer tape
(or duct tape)

Electrical tape

Scissors

Long-nose pliers

Voltage meter
(available online or
at a hardware store)

White glue

Utility knife

Junior hacksaw

Homopolar Motor

A homopolar motor is a super simple electric motor with only one moving part—in this case, a wire. One end has to touch the battery's positive terminal. The other end touches a magnet.

You Will need:

Three circular magnets, roughly the diameter of the battery

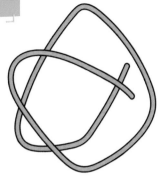

Non-magnetic wire, such as 20-gauge (0.8 mm) uncoated brass wire

AA battery

1. Coil the wire so that it fits loosely around the battery. Double one end over in a hook shape.

2. Stand the battery on the magnets. Now you'll need to reshape the wire to fit. The hooked end rests on the top of the battery, the coil hangs loosely around the battery. The other end of the wire must gently touch the magnets at the bottom. Once you have it just right, the wire will spin around the battery with enthusiasm!

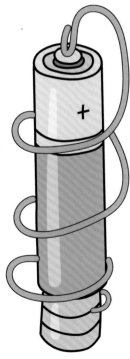

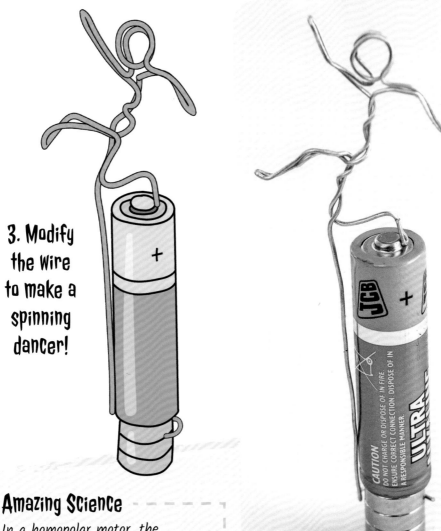

3. Modify the wire to make a spinning dancer!

Amazing Science

In a homopolar motor, the current running through the wire generates a magnetic field (area of magnetism), which makes a magnet move—similar to the more complicated electric motor on the right. In this project, the magnetic field is at a right angle to the field of the disc magnet, so they push against each other to make the wire rotate.

9

Brush Bot

The brush bot is a tiny robot powered by a tiny electric motor. Turn on the bot, and it will scoot around any smooth surface with surprising speed!

You will need:

Toothbrush with bristles the same length

3-volt button battery

Pager motor (3-volt mini vibrating motor)

Tools you will need:
(see page 7)

✭ Double-sided sticky pads
✭ Gaffer tape (or duct tape)
✭ Junior hacksaw

1. Cut the head off the toothbrush with the hacksaw and discard the handle.

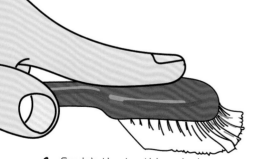

2. Squish the toothbrush down so that the bristles bend in one direction.

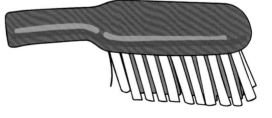

3. The bristles should look something like this—all slightly angled in the same direction.

4. A small pager motor will power the bot and can be purchased from an online supplier for a few dollars.

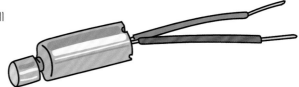

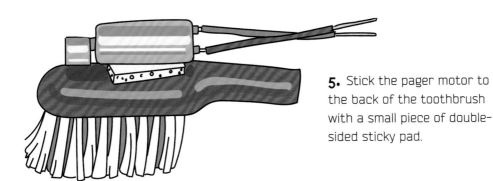

5. Stick the pager motor to the back of the toothbrush with a small piece of double-sided sticky pad.

6. Stick the battery to the neck of the toothbrush with another piece of sticky pad. Insert the red wire between the battery and the pad. The blue wire will be taped to the bottom of the battery.

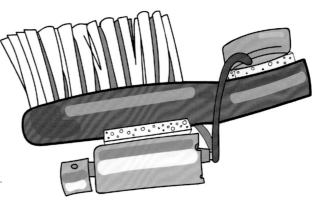

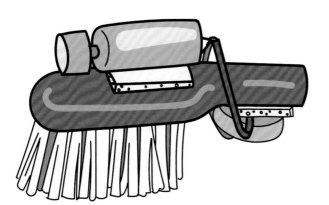

7. Ready for action! Tape the blue wire to the bottom of the battery, and watch the robot go!

8. Make more than one color bot, and race them!

Amazing Science

When English scientist Michael Faraday found that an electric current drives a magnet around and around, he showed how to make an electric motor. Here, the pager motor spins and sets up a vibration in the brush bot. As the bot vibrates, a ratchet effect pushes it backward.

Faraday – Electricity

Mini Lightning

Real lightning is caused by the build-up of static electricity in clouds. This small-scale version uses static electricity from a balloon. It is stored between two layers of alminum foil in a charge storer called a Leyden jar.

You will need:

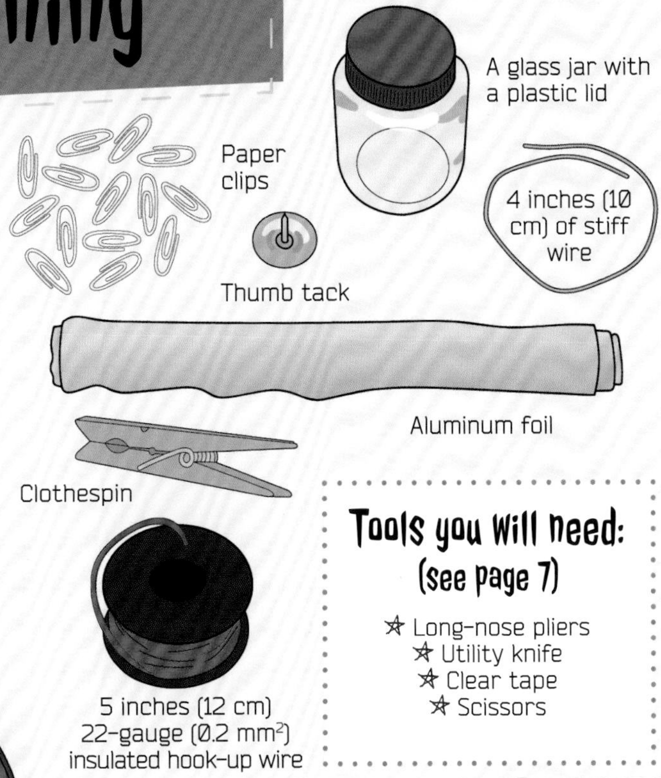

A glass jar with a plastic lid
Paper clips
Thumb tack
4 inches (10 cm) of stiff wire
Aluminum foil
Clothespin
5 inches (12 cm) 22-gauge (0.2 mm²) insulated hook-up wire

Tools you will need:
(see page 7)

☆ Long-nose pliers
☆ Utility knife
☆ Clear tape
☆ Scissors

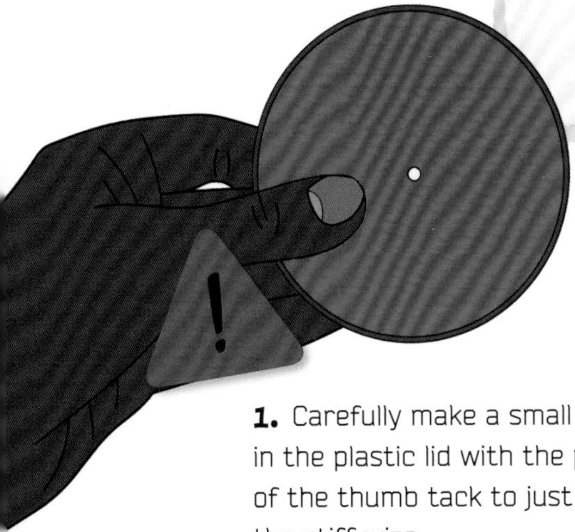

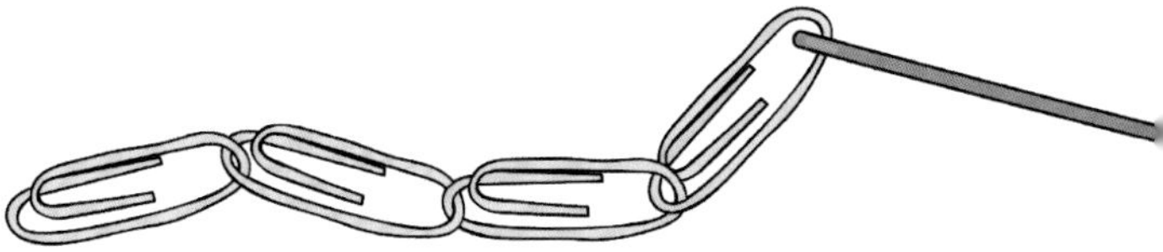

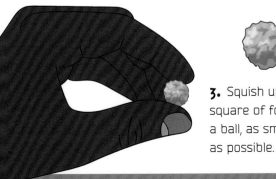

1. Carefully make a small hole in the plastic lid with the point of the thumb tack to just fit the stiff wire.

2. Make a loop at the end of the stiff wire. Add a chain of paper clips.

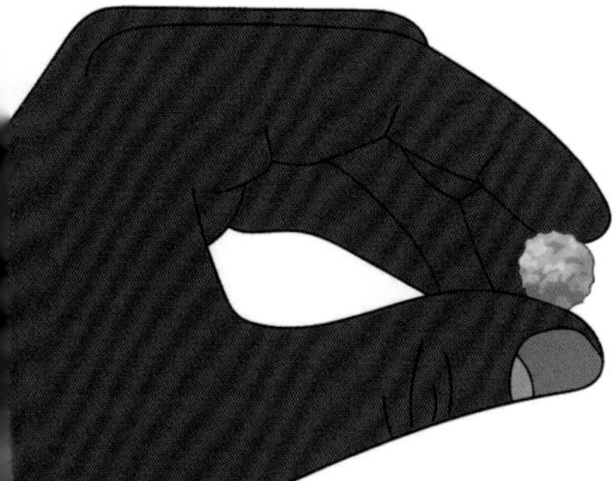

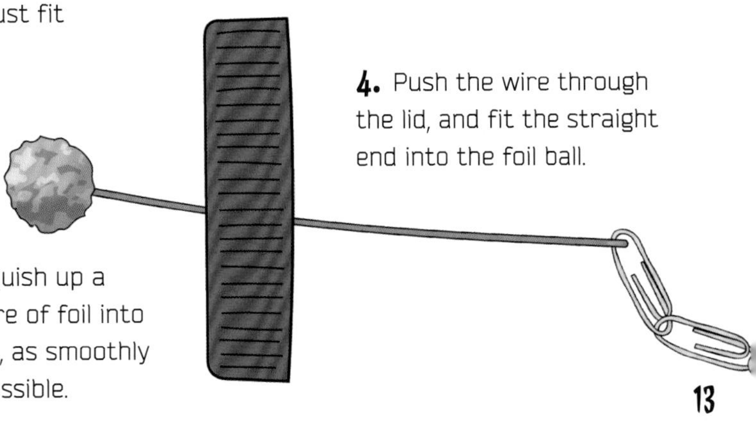

3. Squish up a square of foil into a ball, as smoothly as possible.

4. Push the wire through the lid, and fit the straight end into the foil ball.

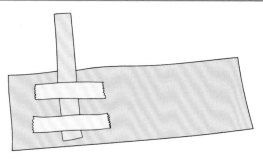

5. Cut two strips of foil that will cover the outside of the jar plus a little extra for overlap. Cut two smaller strips to use for tabs. Use clear tape to attach each smaller tab near the ends of each foil strip.

6. Line the inside of the jar with a foil strip, with the tab lying across the bottom.

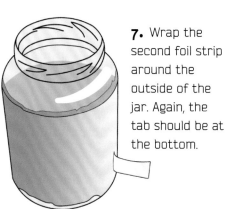

7. Wrap the second foil strip around the outside of the jar. Again, the tab should be at the bottom.

8. Fit the lid on the jar. The paper clip chain should connect the wire to the inner foil tab. The Leyden jar is now complete.

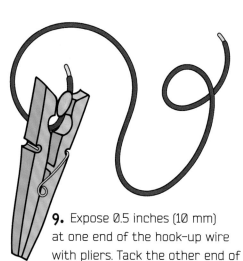

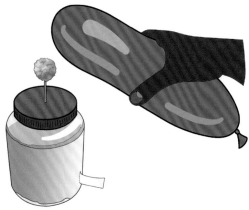

9. Expose 0.5 inches (10 mm) at one end of the hook-up wire with pliers. Tack the other end of the wire to the clothespin with a thumb tack. Clip the clothespin to the outer foil tab on the jar.

10. Charge the Leyden jar by repeatedly rubbing an inflated balloon on your hair, then touching the balloon to the foil ball at the top of the wire. This transfers the static electricity into the jar.

11. Once the jar is charged, bring the end of the flying wire close to the ball and watch the spark jump between them. That's the electricity discharging, or . . .

Lightning!

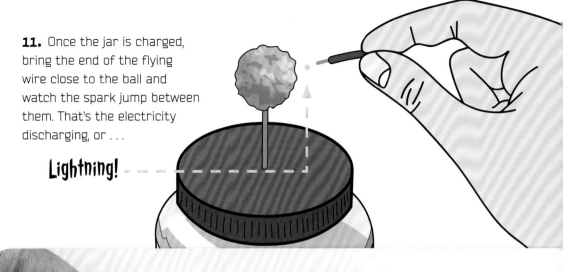

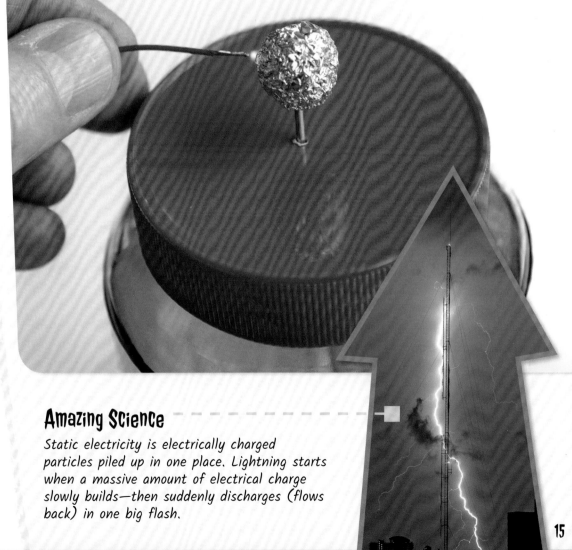

Amazing Science

Static electricity is electrically charged particles piled up in one place. Lightning starts when a massive amount of electrical charge slowly builds—then suddenly discharges (flows back) in one big flash.

Battery Flashlight

You will need:

C battery

Sticky tack

Thumb tacks x2

2.5 inches (60 mm) 22-gauge (0.2 mm²) insulated hook-up wire, red and black x2

Half a plastic egg or a single section from an egg box for the light reflector

Paper clip

2-inch-long (50 mm) wood scrap

1.5-volt bulb

Imagine what it was like in the past when there were only candles to light up the long winter nights! These days we have electricity and bulbs— and we can make this flashlight! Use pliers to expose all the wire ends.

Tools you will need: (see page 7)

✯ Long-nose pliers
✯ Gaffer tape (or duct tape)
✯ Utility knife

1. Make a hole with the utility knife in the bottom of the egg to fit the bulb. Expose the ends of one wire. Twist one end tightly round the bulb. Fit the bulb in place.

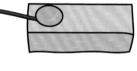

2. Wrap the other end of the wire around a thumb tack, and tack it into the wood.

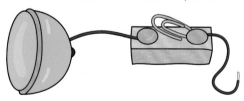

3. Strip the ends of the other wire. Fix the paper clip and one end of the wire to the wood with a thumb tack. The paper clip must not touch the other thumb tack unless it is pressed.

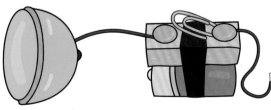

4. Tape the paper clip switch to the battery.

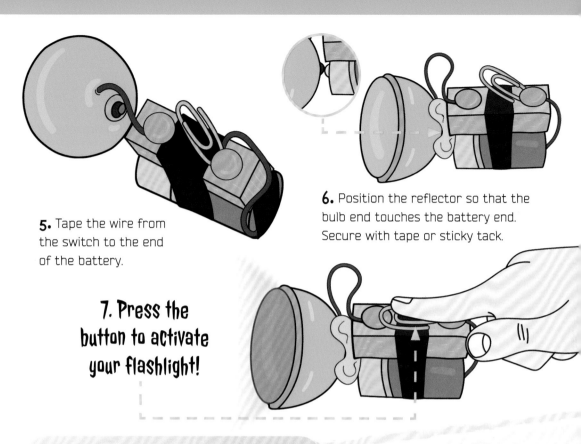

5. Tape the wire from the switch to the end of the battery.

6. Position the reflector so that the bulb end touches the battery end. Secure with tape or sticky tack.

7. Press the button to activate your flashlight!

Amazing Science

An electric current only flows if there is a complete circuit. When the switch is pressed, the circuit is complete. The current then flows from the battery to the lightbulb to make the flashlight shine.

Electromagnet

An electromagnet works when the electricity is turned on. This electromagnet uses a battery to generate a magnetic field. Expose all wire ends by a third of an inch (10 mm) before connecting them to the battery.

You Will need:

¼ x 1 inch (M6 x 25 mm) bolt, steel or nickel-plated steel

Two ⁷⁄₈-inch (20 mm) washers and a ¼-inch (M6) nut, steel or nickel-plated steel

22-gauge (0.2 mm²) insulated hook-up wire, red

C battery

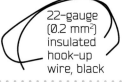
Thumb tacks x3

Strip of cardstock

Paper clip

22-gauge (0.2 mm²) insulated hook-up wire, black

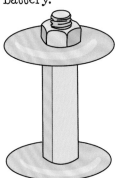
Wood scrap

Tools you will need:
(see page 7)

* ☆ Clear tape
* ☆ Gaffer tape (or duct tape)
* ☆ Electrical tape
* ☆ Long-nose pliers

1. Cut the cardstock to the length of the bolt. Make it into a cylinder. Add one washer to the bolt, add the cylinder, add the second washer and bolt to fasten *(see above)*. This is your magnetic core.

2. Tape the red wire to the cardstock with clear tape as shown, leaving about 6 inches (15 cm) free.

3. Wrap the wire tightly and evenly around the core and secure with tape. This is your electromagnet.

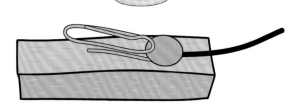

4. For the switch, pin the paper clip to the wood with a thumb tack while connecting it to 6 inches (15 cm) of black wire.

6. Connect a 6-inch (15 cm) length of black wire under a second thumb tack. The paper clip must only touch the second thumb tack when pressed down *(right)*.

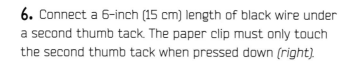

7. Using gaffer tape, secure the wires from electromagnet and switch to the battery. Join the loose wire ends with electrical tape as shown.

8. The circuit is ready! Press the switch to turn on the electromagnet.

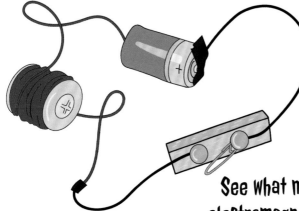

See What materials the electromagnet Will attract!

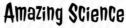

Amazing Science

An electric current creates its own magnetic field. Here, the bolt concentrates the wire's magnetic field. It is strengthened further each time the wire is wrapped round the bolt. This is why electromagnets can be very strong.

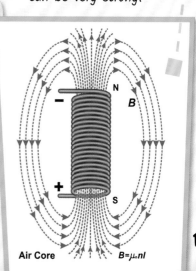

N

B

−

+

S

Air Core $B = \mu_0 nI$

Telegraph

Make the pushbutton switch and electromagnet coil on pp. 18–19. Expose the ends of the wires by a third of an inch (10 mm) before connecting them.

⅞-inch (20 mm) steel washer

Coffee stirrer cut to 2.7 inches (70 mm)

2-inch-long (50 mm) wood scraps x2

22-gauge (0.2 mm²) insulated hook-up wire (for a long-distance telegraph!)

Tools you will need:
(see page 7)

✱ Sticky foam pads
✱ Gaffer tape (or duct tape)
✱ Electrical tape
✱ White glue
✱ Junior hacksaw

Before radio and telephones existed, the fastest way to communicate long-distance was by telegraph. The telegraph operator tapped a message in Morse code on the switch, and the receiver translated the clicks back into the message. You can try sending a message to another room. To do this, splice in two 10-foot (3 m) lengths of wire to your original circuit, one on either side, by twisting the exposed ends together. Tape the joins.

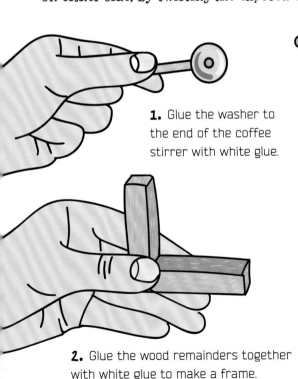

1. Glue the washer to the end of the coffee stirrer with white glue.

2. Glue the wood remainders together with white glue to make a frame.

3. Use sticky foam pads to stick the electromagnet coil to the frame. Use thumb tacks to fit the washer assembly into position so that it is just above the bolt.

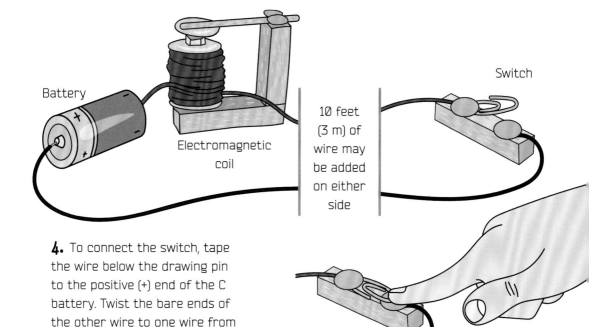

Battery

Electromagnetic coil

10 feet (3 m) of wire may be added on either side

Switch

4. To connect the switch, tape the wire below the drawing pin to the positive (+) end of the C battery. Twist the bare ends of the other wire to one wire from the coil and cover with electrical tape. Tape the other coil wire to the other end of the battery.

5. Tap out your Morse Code message on the button.

It will be received as clicks on the telegraph.

Amazing Science

The telegraph works by switching on a current as each letter is tapped. As you tap on your telegraph, electricity flows down the wire into the electromagnet. It attracts the metal washer to make the long and short clicks.

Jumping Toys

You will need:

Tissue paper

A balloon

. . . and your hair!

Cut out figure shapes from the tissue paper. Rub the balloon on your hair to charge it up with static electricity. Spread the tissue paper people out on a flat surface. Bring the balloon close to them and watch them jump up! With care, you will be able to make them dance on your work surface.

Amazing Science

Positive and negative electrical charges attract each other. The balloon has a negative charge from your hair, which is opposite to the charge on the tissue paper people, so it pulls them towards it.

Bending Water

A balloon and
a running tap

Static electricity can be used
to bend a stream of water!

1. Turn on a tap so that the
water is running in a steady
stream.

2. Charge up an inflated
balloon by rubbing it on your
hair. Bring the balloon close
to the stream of water but
not touching it. The water will
be attracted to the
balloon and form a
gentle curve!

3. Try charging up
other materials and
see what works best
for water-bending!

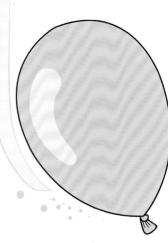

Amazing Science

*Water has both positive
and negative charges. The
negatively-charged balloon
repels the negative particles
in the water, pushing them
to the opposite side of the
stream. So the side of the
stream closer to the balloon
becomes slightly positive.
This positively charged water
is attracted to the balloon.*

23

Charge Power

There are many ways a static electrical charge can build up, but how do you detect it? The answer is: with an electroscope made from a few household items.

Large jar

Plastic lid to fit or cover the jar

Sticky tack

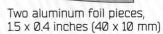

Two aluminum foil pieces, 1.5 x 0.4 inches (40 x 10 mm)

20-gauge 0.8 mm uncoated brass wire

Tools you will need:
(see page 7)
✭ Utility knife

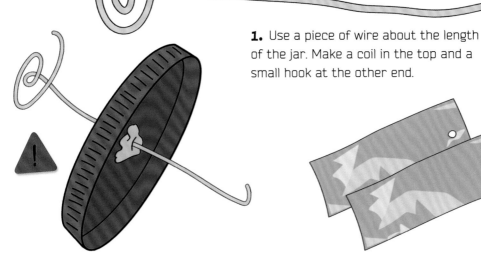

1. Use a piece of wire about the length of the jar. Make a coil in the top and a small hook at the other end.

2. Make a hole in the plastic lid with a utility knife. Thread the wire through, and secure it with sticky tack.

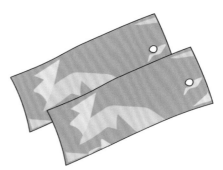

3. At one end of the two foil pieces, make a small hole just big enough for the wire.

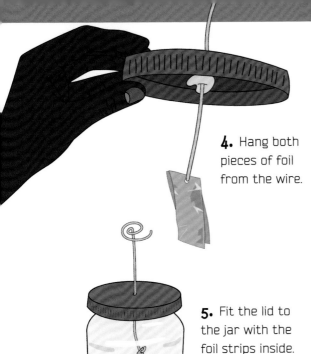

4. Hang both pieces of foil from the wire.

5. Fit the lid to the jar with the foil strips inside. The foil must not touch the sides of the jar.

6. Your electroscope is complete!

Charge up a balloon by rubbing it on your hair then bring it close to the wire spiral. The foil strips will move apart, showing the presence of electricity.

Amazing Science

In this electroscope, the amount the foil strips move apart indicates how much repulsion there is between like charges. The farther apart the foil strips, the greater the strength of the static electrical charge.

LED Light

These magnetic LED lights stick to any metal surface and will work for days before the battery finally runs out!

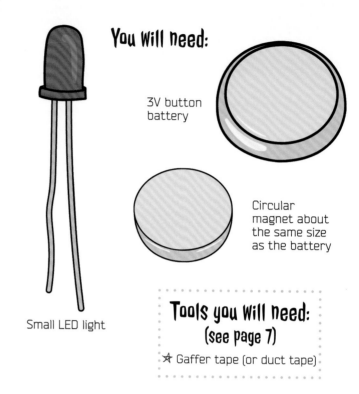

You will need:

3V button battery

Circular magnet about the same size as the battery

Small LED light

Tools you will need:
(see page 7)

★ Gaffer tape (or duct tape)

1. Fit the magnet to the battery. The legs of the LED straddle the battery and magnet, one on each side. Make sure that you have the legs positioned correctly: the longer leg goes to the positive (+) terminal of the battery.

2. If it doesn't work, try flipping the battery over. Then wrap it with a bit of tape to hold the LED in place.

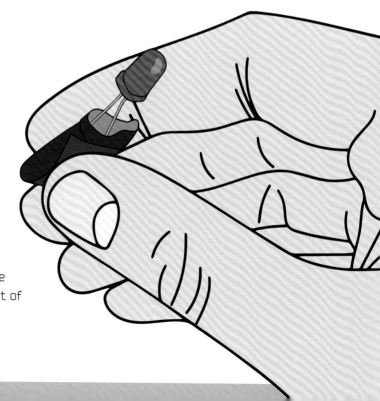

3. Find a suitable place for your LED light!

Try the fridge, the back of the car, or see if you can throw it up to stick to some scaffolding!

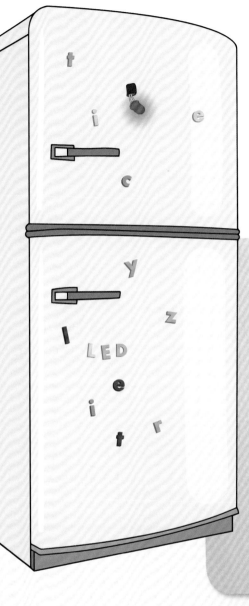

Amazing Science

LED stands for light emitting diode. A diode is an electronic component that allows electricity to flow in only one direction. The LED must be connected correctly or it won't light up.

Potato Power

Did you know that you can power a light with electricity from a potato? Here's how . . .

Potatoes x3

2-inch (50 mm) copper pieces, such as cuttings from pipe x3

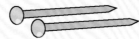

Zinc-plated roof nails x3

LED light

22-gauge (0.2 mm²) insulated hook-up wire lengths with bare ends

Tools you will need: (see page 7)

✷ Voltage meter

Clothespins x6

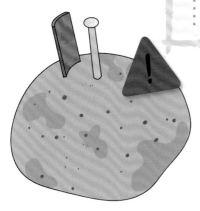

1. Push your zinc and copper pieces into a potato close together but not touching.

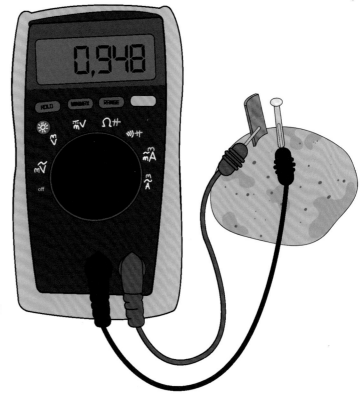

2. With a voltage meter you will be able to measure the electricity being generated by the potato.

3. Use four 4-inch (100 mm) lengths of wire and clothespins to connect three potatoes in series. Connect the zinc on one to the copper on the next and so on.

The two extreme ends can then be used to light your LED!

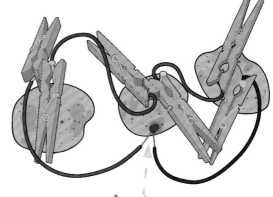

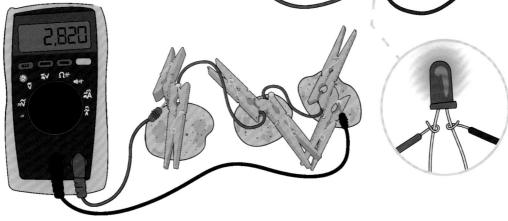

4. Check out the voltage on those 'taters!

Amazing Science

All you need to make an electric battery is two different metals: one for the anode (positive terminal), the other for the cathode (negative). You also need a substance called an electrolyte. This can even be a potato, which produces enough electricity to light an LED.

Glossary

charged particle:
A particle, or tiny piece of matter, that has an electrical charge. The charge is either positive or negative. An atom is a particle made of even smaller particles called protons, neutrons, and electrons. Protons have a positive charge, neutrons have no charge, and electrons have a negative charge.

electric circuit:
A complete path carrying an electric current, powered by a battery or other current source. Switching on a light, for example, completes the circuit so the current goes straight to the light bulb to give it the power to work.

electromagnet:
A magnet made from a coil of wire wrapped around an iron core and connected to a battery. When the current is running through the wire, it creates a magnetic field just like the one around a bar magnet. The wire coil makes the magnetic field stronger. But switching off the current on an electromagnet switches off the magnetism.

Leyden jar:
A glass jar with metal foil on the inside and outside, used for storing static electricity and conducting experiments.

magnet:
Typically a bar of magnetic metal, such as iron, with a north and a south pole where the magnetism is strongest. Opposite poles attract each other, like poles repel each other. A magnet creates an invisible field of force around it called a magnetic field, which attracts other magnets or magnetic materials.

static electricity:
An imbalance of positive and negative charges in or on a material. These charges build up until they can be released. So if you have a build-up of negatively charged electrons, they will jump over to a positively charged thing (or person) when they meet. This gives you a shock.

Did You Know?

* Some animals have a magnetic substance called magnetite in their bodies. Homing pigeons have it in their beaks, and it may help them to navigate.

* Magnets can lift cars, but the world's most powerful magnet, at Los Alamos Laboratory in New Mexico, is about 50 times more powerful than those.

* The electricity used in homes alternates, or switches direction, about 50 times a second.

* Electricity travels at 95 percent the speed of light through a copper wire.

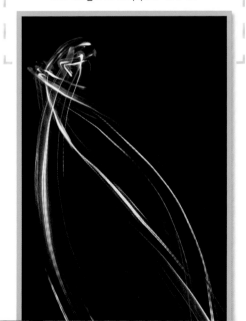

* A bolt of lightning can measure up to 3,000,000 volts, reach 54,000°F (30,000°C), and lasts a fraction of a second.

* An electric eel can give a shock of 500 volts.

31

Index

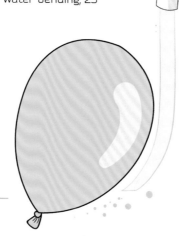
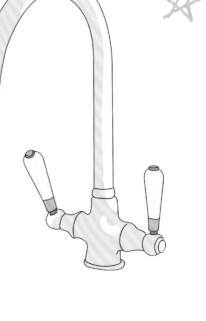

The Author

Rob Ives is a former math and science teacher, now a designer and paper engineer living in Cumbria, UK. He creates science- and project-based children's books, including *Paper Models that Rock!* and *Paper Automata*. He specializes in character-based paper animations and all kinds of fun and fascinating science projects, and he often visits schools to talk about design technology and demonstrate his models.

The Illustrator

Eva Sassin is a freelance illustrator born in London, UK. She has always loved illustrating, whether it be scary, fun monsters or cute, sparkly fairies. She carries a sketchbook everywhere, but she has even drawn on the back of receipts if she's forgotten it! In her free time, she travels around London to visit exhibitions and small cafés where she enjoys sketching up new ideas and characters. She is also a massive film buff!

Picture Credits (abbreviations: t = top; b = bottom; c = center; l = left; r = right)
© www.shutterstock.com:

9 br, 12 bl, 15 br, 17 br, 19 br, 21 br, 22 bl, 23 br, 25 br, 27 br, 29 br, 31 tl, 31 cr, 31 bl.